hide this italian book for lovers

Berlitz Publishing

New York   Munich   Singapore

Hide This Italian Book for Lovers

Contacting the Editors
Every effort has been made to provide accurate information in this publication, but changes are inevitable. The publisher cannot be responsible for any resulting loss, inconvenience or injury. We would appreciate it if readers would call our attention to any errors or outdated information by contacting Berlitz Publishing, 193 Morris Avenue, Springfield, NJ 07081, USA. email: comments@berlitzbooks.com

Second Printing: February 2007
Printed in China

Writer: Nadja Rizzuti
Publishing Director: Sheryl Olinsky Borg
Senior Editor/Project Manager: Lorraine Sova
Editor: Emily Bernath
Cover and Interior Design: Wee Design Group, Blair Swick
Production Manager: Elizabeth Gaynor
Illustrations: Kyle Webster, Amy Zaleski

Hide This Italian Book for lovers has everything from cheesy pick-up lines to erotic sex talk. "Hot" words are labeled with 🌡️ and the hottest language with 🌡️. Go ahead—get hot 'n heavy with Italian.

table of contents

Vieni spesso
da queste parti?

vee-<u>eh</u>-nee <u>spehs</u>-soh dah <u>kweh</u>steh <u>pah</u>rtee

hooking up

Come here often?

It sounds better in Italian.

hooking up

Sei s♂lo?

say <u>sohloh</u>

Sei s♀la?

say <u>sohlah</u>

hooking up

Are you alone?

Make sure that guy or girl you're after isn't taken.

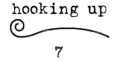

hooking up

Posso offrirti qualcosa da bere?

<u>pohs</u>-soh ohf-<u>freer</u>tee kwahl-<u>kohz</u>ah dah <u>beh</u>reh

Can I buy you a drink?

A typical line—but it works every time.

hooking up

Ti va di ballare?

tee vah dee bahl-<u>lah</u>reh

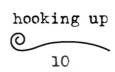

hooking up

10

Wanna dance?

An ideal way to get close to someone.

hooking up

Ti accompagno a casa?

tee ahk-koh<u>mpah</u>nyoh ah <u>kah</u>zah

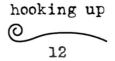

Can I take you home?

Get some alone time.

hooking up

13

hooking up

14

the Scoop

Say "sei bellissima ♀/ bellissimo ♂" you're beautiful, or "hai degli occhi bellissimi", you have beautiful eyes, and the person you're trying to pick up will roll his or her eyes in disappointment. Italians consider these over-used lines to be really corny. Instead, be honest and direct—Italians will be flattered by someone who can express his or her feelings sincerely.

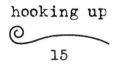

Che maschio♂!

keh <u>mahs</u>key-oh

Che femmina♀!

keh <u>fehm</u>-mee-nah

What a hottie!

Literally: What a male!
What a female!

Che figo♂!

keh <u>fee</u>goh

Che figa♀!

keh <u>fee</u>gah

What a sexy guy!

What a sexy girl!

hooking up

20

Food + sex = "figa". Some speculate that "figa", a northern Italian variant of "fico", fig, became a slang word for vulva because of the similarities in shape between the two. Don't use the term liberally: it's vulgar in some regions of Italy. Try not to confuse "figa" with "fico" or "figo"—both of which mean cool!

È una gnocca da paura.

eh <u>oo</u>nah <u>nyohk</u>-kah dah pah-<u>oo</u>rah

She's a totally hot woman.

*"Una gnocca" is,
literally, a potato dumpling.*

*Guys: Say this to your buddies
but don't say it to a woman—
it's offensive.*

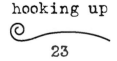

hooking up

23

Troppo carino ♂!

trohp-poh ka<u>ree</u>noh

Troppo carina ♀!

trohp-poh ka<u>ree</u>nah

hooking up

24

Totally cute!

Watch your tone of voice
when saying this—
you wouldn't want it
to come across as sarcastic.

hooking up

Baciami!

bahchah-mee

kisses & hugs

Kiss me!

Ah, instant gratification...

kisses & hugs

Me lo dai un bacio?

meh loh <u>dah</u>-ee oon <u>bah</u>-choh

kisses & hugs

28

Give me a kiss?

Who would say no?!

kisses & hugs

Abbracciami!

ahb-<u>brah</u>-chah-mee

kisses & hugs

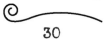

30

Let's cuddle!

Need some physical attention?

kisses & hugs

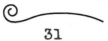

kisses & hugs

32

the Scoop

True or false: Italian guys are macho. Answer: Falsc! The myth of the macho Italian male who's interested in hooking up as much as possible isn't accurate. Italian guys are into sports and friendship as much as they're into girls—and the same can be said about Italian women. It's only your "nonna", grandma, who still thinks that guys are only after one thing...

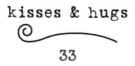

kisses & hugs

Ho voglia di te!

oh <u>voh</u>-lyah dee teh

I want you!

kisses & hugs

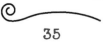

Cos'è...
un succhiotto?

kohzeh... oon sook-key-oht-toh

Is that... a hickey?

Thought you could cover it up, huh?!

kisses & hugs

Fa' *l'amore* con me.

fah lah<u>moh</u>reh kohn meh

Make *love* to me.

A romantic way to say it.

kisses & hugs

kisses & hugs

40

the scoop

Privacy may be an issue for some young Italian couples. Italians usually live at home with mom and/or dad well into their late 20s—some even longer. So, couples have to be pretty creative about finding some alone time. Lovers make time for each other in parked cars and other semi-secluded spots: the beach, the mountains, the woods. There's always a chance that they'll get caught in the act, but that makes it all the more exciting!

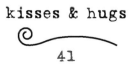

kisses & hugs

Ci facciamo delle storie.

chee fah-<u>chah</u>moh <u>dehl</u>-leh <u>stoh</u>ree-eh

kisses & hugs

We're just seeing each other.

Literally: We have some stories.

Abbiamo una tresca.

ahb-bee<u>ah</u>moh <u>oo</u>nah <u>treh</u>skah

We're having an affair.

Enjoy sex—without the commitment!

kisses & hugs

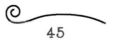

Stiamo uscendo.

stee-<u>ah</u>moh oo<u>shehn</u>-doh

We're dating. ♥

Serious stuff, huh?

kisses & hugs

47

È il mio ragazzo♂.

eh eel <u>mee</u>-oh rahgah-tzoh

È la mia ragazza♀.

eh lah <u>mee</u>-ah rahgah-tzah

He's my boyfriend.

She's my girlfriend.

Let everyone know!

kisses & hugs

Siamo *amanti.*

see-<u>ah</u>moh ah<u>mah</u>ntee

kisses & hugs

50

We're *lovers.*

With all the fringe benefits...

kisses & hugs

51

Siamo innamoratissimi.

see-<u>ah</u>moh een-nahmoh-rah<u>tees</u>-seemee

We're deeply in *love*.

First comes love, then comes...

kisses & hugs

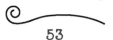

Hai voglia di divertirti?

ahee <u>voh</u>-lyah dee deevehr-<u>teer</u>tee

Do you wanna "party"?

All night long?

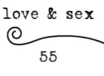

love & sex

Ti mangerei di baci!

tee mahnjeh-<u>reh</u>-ee dee <u>bah</u>-chee

love & sex

56

I could just eat you up!

He or she is delicious, huh?!

love & sex

Andiamo in camera, ti va?

ahndee-<u>ah</u>moh een <u>kah</u>mehrah tee vah

love & sex

Wanna go to
the bedroom?

You're not tired, are you?!

love & sex

Ti va un massaggio?

tee vah oon mahs-<u>sah</u>-djoh

Can I give you a massage?

Foot, neck, back... take your pick!

love & sex

61

Non sai cosa ti farei.

nohn <u>sah-ee</u> <u>koh</u>zah
tee fah-<u>ray</u>

Guess what I'm going to do to you.

Something kinky, right?

love & sex

Spogliati.

<u>spohl</u>yahtee

love & sex

64

Get undressed.

Is this a command?!

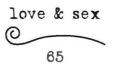

love & sex

65

Facciamo sesso.

fah-<u>chah</u>moh <u>sehs</u>-soh

love & sex

Let's have sex.

No foolin' around...

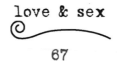

love & sex

Dimmi le cosaccie.

deem-mee leh koh<u>zah</u>-cheh

love & sex

Talk dirty to me.

Whatever puts you in the mood.

love & sex

Facciamolo strano.

fah-<u>chahmoh</u>-loh <u>strahnoh</u>

love & sex

Let's get kinky.

Literally: Let's do it in a weird way.

love & sex

love & sex

the scoop

Ever heard the expression, "Italians do it better"? The saying is based in some truth—many Italians do enjoy having sex and they enjoy talking about it too. Guys and girls have been known to brag about the number of times they've had sex in one night (with the same person, of course). Well, "practice makes perfect"!

Dove ho messo il mio vibratore?

dohveh oh <u>mehs</u>-soh eel <u>mee</u>-oh veebrah-<u>toh</u>reh

love & sex

Where's my vibrator?

Toys are fun.

love & sex

Metti qualcosa di sexy!

meht-tee kwahl-<u>koh</u>zah dee <u>sehk</u>-see

Put on something sexy!

Any suggestions?

love & sex

Guardiamo un film porno?

gwahr-dee-<u>ah</u>moh oon feelm <u>pohr</u>noh

love & sex

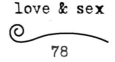

78

Wanna watch a porno?

You need to do something to pass the time!

love & sex

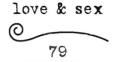

79

Hai un preservativo?

<u>a</u>hee oon prehzehr-vah<u>tee</u>voh

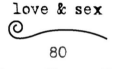

love & sex

80

Do you have condoms?

That's a forward question, isn't it?

love & sex

81

A che gusto lo vuoi il preservativo?

ah keh <u>goo</u>stoh loh voo-<u>oh</u>ee eel prehzehr-vah<u>tee</u>voh

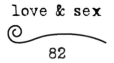

Which flavor (condom) do you want to use?

Cherry, chocolate, or coconut?

Toccami!

tohk-kah-mee

love & sex

84

Touch me!

Go ahead.

Ti piace così?

tee pee-<u>ah</u>cheh koh<u>zee</u>

love & sex

86

Does that feel good?

Sure does.

love & sex

Hai qualche fantasia sessuale?

ahee kwahlkeh fahntah-zee-ah sehs-soo-ahleh

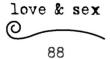

love & sex

88

Do you have any sexual fantasies?

What do you have in mind?

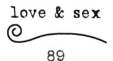
love & sex

89

Abbiamo fatto sesso.

ahb-bee<u>ah</u>moh <u>faht</u>-toh <u>sehs</u>-soh

love & sex

90

We had sex.

Simple and straightforward.

love & sex

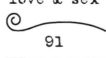

91

Siamo andati
a letto insieme.

see-<u>ah</u>moh ahn<u>dah</u>tee ah <u>leht</u>-toh eensee-<u>eh</u>meh

love & sex

We slept together.

Did you actually get some sleep?
Hope not!

love & sex

93

Abbiamo passato la notte insieme.

ahb-bee<u>ah</u>moh pahs-<u>sah</u>toh
lah <u>noht</u>-teh eensee-<u>eh</u>meh

love & sex

94

We spent the night together.

Lucky you!

love & sex

95

Ti *amo.*

tee <u>ah</u>moh

I *love* you.

Ah, Italian romance...

u + me 4ever

Mi piace come fai *l'amore*.

me pee-<u>ah</u>cheh <u>koh</u>meh <u>fah</u>-ee lah<u>moh</u>reh

u + me 4ever

98

I like the way you make *love* to me.

Give him or her an ego boost.

u + me 4ever

Sei fantastico♂!

say fahn<u>tah</u>-steekoh

Sei fantastica♀!

say fahn<u>tah</u>-steekah

You're good (in bed)!

Thanks for the compliment.

Sono stato ♂
benissimo.

sohnoh stahtoh behnees-seemoh

Sono stata ♀
benissimo.

sohnoh stahtah behnees-seemoh

u + me 4ever

I had a great time
with you (last night).

u + me 4ever

103

Chiamami.

key-<u>ah</u>mahmee

u + me 4ever

104

Call me.

Cross your fingers that

he or she does...

Quando ci rivediamo?

<u>kwahn</u>doh chee reevehdee-<u>ah</u>moh

u + me 4ever

When can I see you again?

Don't act desperate.

u + me 4ever

107

Non posso vivere senza di te.

nohn <u>pohs</u>-soh <u>vee</u>vehreh <u>sehn</u>tzah dee teh

u + me 4ever

108

I can't live without you.

You're obsessed!

u + me 4ever

109

Vieni a vivere con me.

vee-<u>eh</u>-nee ah <u>vee</u>vehreh kohn meh

u + me 4ever

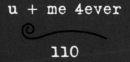

110

Move in with me.

Pack your bags and go.

Sposami.

<u>spoh</u>zahmee

u + me 4ever

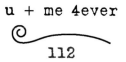

112

Marry me.

Where's the ring?!

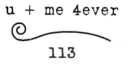

Sono incinta.

sohnoh eencheentah

u + me 4ever

I'm pregnant.

Ah, family...

u + me 4ever

amore mio

ah<u>moh</u>reh <u>mee</u>-oh

my love

Say this to your soul mate.

darling

A popular term of endearment...

cucciolo ♂

koo-choh-loh

cucciola ♀

koo-choh-lah

sweet talk

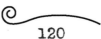

120

my pet

Literally: puppy

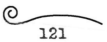

tesoro

teh<u>zoh</u>roh

dear

Literally: treasure

dolcezza

dohl-<u>cheh</u>-tzah

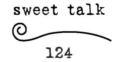

honey

Is he or she just delicious?

sweet talk

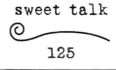

125

sweet talk

126

the scoop

You could end an Italian fling with "rimaniamo amici", let's just be friends, but most Italians won't take you up on your offer. Friendship after romance is pretty much a no-no in Italy, especially if a new boyfriend or girlfriend enters the picture. If someone breaks up with you, he or she will probably be blunt: "è finita", it's over (between us)!

fine